COUNTRY

Formal Name: Republic of the Philippines (Republika ng Pilipinas).

Short Form: Philippines (Pilipinas).

Term for Citizen(s): Filipino(s).

Capital: Manila.

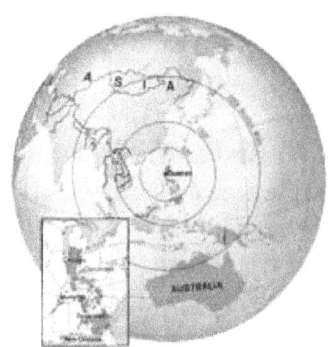

Click to Enlarge Image

Major Cities: Located on Luzon Island, Metropolitan Manila, including the adjacent Quezon City and surrounding suburbs, is the largest city in the Philippines, with about 12 million people, or nearly 14 percent of the total population. Other large cities include Cebu City on Cebu Island and Davao City on Mindanao Island.

Independence: The Philippines attained independence from Spain on June 12, 1898, and from the United States on July 4, 1946.

Public Holidays: New Year's Day (January 1), Holy Thursday (also called Maundy Thursday, movable date in March or April), Good Friday (movable date in March or April), Araw ng Kagitingan (Day of Valor, commonly called Bataan Day outside of the Philippines, April 9), Labor Day (May 1), Independence Day (June 12), National Heroes Day (last Sunday of August), Bonifacio Day (celebration of the birthday of Andres Bonifacio, November 30), Eid al Fitr (the last day of Ramadan, movable date), Christmas Day (December 25), Rizal Day (the date of the execution by the Spanish of José Rizal in 1896, December 30).

Flag: The flag of the Philippines has two equal horizontal bands of blue (top) and red with a white equilateral triangle based on the hoist side; in the center of the triangle is a yellow sun with eight primary rays (each containing three individual rays), and in each corner of the triangle is a small yellow five-pointed star.

Click to Enlarge Image

HISTORICAL BACKGROUND

Early History: The Philippine archipelago was settled at least 30,000 years ago, when migrations from the Indonesian archipelago and elsewhere are believed to have occurred. Additional migrations took place over the next millennia. Over time, social and political organization developed and evolved in the widely scattered islands. The basic unit of settlement was the *barangay* (a Malay word for boat that came to be used to denote a communal settlement). Kinship groups were led by a *datu* (chief), and within the *barangay* there were broad social divisions consisting of nobles, freemen, and dependent and landless agricultural workers and slaves. Over the centuries, Indo-Malay migrants were joined by Chinese traders. A major development in the early period was the introduction of Islam to the Philippines by traders and proselytizers from the Indonesian islands. By A.D. 1500, Islam had been established in the Sulu Archipelago and spread from there to Mindanao; it reached the Manila area by 1565. In the midst of the introduction of Islam came the introduction of Christianity, with the arrival of the Spanish.

Spanish Control: Ferdinand Magellan was the first European recorded to have landed in the Philippines. He arrived in March 1521 during his circumnavigation of the globe. He claimed land for the king of Spain but was killed by a local chief. Following several more Spanish expeditions, the first permanent settlement was established in Cebu in 1565. After defeating a local Muslim ruler, the Spanish set up their capital at Manila in 1571, and they named their new colony after King Philip II of Spain. In doing so, the Spanish sought to acquire a share in the lucrative spice trade, develop better contacts with China and Japan, and gain converts to Christianity. Only the third objective was eventually realized. As with other Spanish colonies, church and state became inseparably linked in carrying out Spanish objectives. Several Roman Catholic religious orders were assigned the responsibility of Christianizing the local population. The civil administration built upon the traditional village organization and used traditional local leaders to rule indirectly for Spain. Through these efforts, a new cultural community was developed, but Muslims (known as Moros by the Spanish) and upland tribal peoples remained detached and alienated.

Trade in the Philippines centered around the "Manila galleons," which sailed from Acapulco on the west coast of Mexico (New Spain) with shipments of silver bullion and minted coin that were exchanged for return cargoes of Chinese goods, mainly silk textiles and porcelain. There was no direct trade with Spain and little exploitation of indigenous natural resources. Most investment was in the galleon trade. But, as this trade thrived, another unwelcome element was introduced—sojourning Chinese entrepreneurs and service providers.

During the Seven Years' War (1756–63), British East India Company forces captured Manila. Although the Philippines was returned to Spain at the end of the war, the British occupation marked the beginning of the end of the old order. Rebellions broke out in the north, and while the Spanish were busy fighting the British, Moros raided from the south. The Chinese community, resentful of Spanish discrimination, supported the British with laborers and armed men. The restoration of Spanish rule brought reforms aimed at promoting the economic development of the islands and making them independent of subsidies from New Spain. The galleon trade ceased in 1815, and from that date onward the Royal Company of the Philippines, which had been chartered in 1785, promoted direct and tariff-free trade between the islands and Spain. Cash crops were cultivated for trade with Europe and Latin America, but profits diminished after Spain's Latin American colonies became independent in the 1810s and 1820s. In 1834 the Royal Company of the Philippines was abolished, and free trade was formally recognized. With its excellent harbor, Manila became an open port for Asian, European, and North American traders. In 1873 additional ports were opened to foreign commerce, and by the late nineteenth century three crops—tobacco, abaca, and sugar—dominated Philippine exports.

Rise of Nationalism: Also in the late nineteenth century, Chinese immigration, now with official approval, increased, and Chinese mestizos became a feature in Filipino social and economic life. So, too, did the growing Filipino native elite class of *ilustrados* (literally, enlightened ones), who became increasingly receptive to liberal and democratic ideas. Conservative Catholic friars continued to dominate the Spanish establishment, however. They resisted the inclusion of native clergy and were economically secure, with their large land holdings and control of churches, schools, and other establishments. Despite the bias against native priests, brothers, and nuns, some members of Filipino religious orders became prominent to the point of leading local religious movements and even insurrections against the establishment. Additionally, *ilustrados* returning from education and exile abroad brought new ideas that merged with folk religion to spur a national resistance.

One of the early nationalist leaders was José Rizal, a physician, scientist, scholar, and writer. His writings as a member of the Propaganda Movement (intellectually active, upper-class Filipino reformers) had a considerable impact on the awakening of the Filipino national consciousness. His books were banned, and he lived in self-imposed exile. Rizal returned from overseas in 1892 to found the Liga Filipina (Philippine League), a national, nonviolent political organization, but he was arrested and exiled and the league dissolved. One result was the split of the nationalist movement between the reform-minded *ilustrados* and a more revolutionary and independence-minded plebeian constituency. Many of the latter joined the Katipunan, a secret society founded by Andres Bonifacio in 1892 and committed to winning national independence. By 1896, the year the Katipunan rose in revolt against Spain, it had 30,000 members. Although Rizal, who had again returned to the Philippines, was not a member of the Katipunan, he was arrested and executed on December 30, 1896, for his alleged role in the rebellion. With Rizal's martyrdom, the rebels, led by Emilio Aguinaldo as president, were filled with new determination. Spanish troops defeated the insurgents, however, and Aguinaldo and his government went into exile in Hong Kong in December 1897.

When the Spanish-American War broke out in April 1898, Spain's fleet was easily defeated at Manila. Aguinaldo returned, and his 12,000 troops kept the Spanish forces bottled up in Manila until U.S. troops landed. The Spanish cause was doomed, but the Americans did nothing to accommodate the inclusion of Aguinaldo in the succession. Fighting between American and Filipino troops broke out almost as soon as the Spanish had been defeated. Aguinaldo issued a declaration of independence on June 12, 1898. However, the Treaty of Paris, signed on December 10, 1898, by the United States and Spain, ceded the Philippines, Guam, and Puerto Rico to the United States, recognized Cuban independence, and gave US$20 million to Spain. A revolutionary congress convened at Malolos, north of Manila, promulgated a constitution on January 21, 1899, and inaugurated Aguinaldo as president of the new republic two days later. Hostilities broke out in February 1899, and by March 1901 Aguinaldo had been captured and his forces defeated. Despite Aguinaldo's call to his compatriots to lay down their arms, insurgent resistance continued until 1903. The Moros, suspicious of both the Christian Filipino insurgents and the Americans, remained largely neutral, but eventually their own armed resistance had to be subjugated, and Moro territory was placed under U.S. military rule until 1914.

United States Rule: U.S. rule over the Philippines had two phases. The first phase was from 1898 to 1935, during which time Washington defined its colonial mission as one of tutelage and preparing the Philippines for eventual independence. Political organizations developed quickly, and the popularly elected Philippine Assembly (lower house) and the U.S.-appointed Philippine Commission (upper house) served as a bicameral legislature. The *ilustrados* formed the Federalista Party, but their statehood platform had limited appeal. In 1905 the party was renamed the National Progressive Party and took up a platform of independence. The Nacionalista Party was formed in 1907 and dominated Filipino politics until after World War II. Its leaders were not ilustrados. Despite their "immediate independence" platform, the party leaders participated in a collaborative leadership with the United States. A major development emerging in the post-World War I period was resistance to elite control of the land by tenant farmers, who were supported by the Socialist Party and the Communist Party of the Philippines. Tenant strikes and occasional violence occurred as the Great Depression wore on and cash-crop prices collapsed.

The second period of United States rule—from 1936 to 1946—was characterized by the establishment of the Commonwealth of the Philippines and occupation by Japan during World War II. Legislation passed by the U.S. Congress in 1934 provided for a 10-year period of transition to independence. The country's first constitution was framed in 1934 and overwhelmingly approved by plebiscite in 1935, and Manuel Quezon was elected president of the commonwealth. Quezon later died in exile in 1944 and was succeeded by Vice President Sergio Osme□a. Japan attacked the Philippines on December 8, 1941, and occupied Manila on January 2, 1942. Tokyo set up an ostensibly independent republic, which was opposed by underground and guerrilla activity that eventually reached large-scale proportions. A major element of the resistance in the Central Luzon area was furnished by the Huks (short for Hukbalahap, or People's Anti-Japanese Army). Allied forces invaded the Philippines in October 1944, and the Japanese surrendered on September 2, 1945.

Early Independence Period: World War II had been demoralizing for the Philippines, and the islands suffered from rampant inflation and shortages of food and other goods. Various trade and security issues with the United States also remained to be settled before Independence Day. The Allied leaders wanted to purge officials who collaborated with the Japanese during the war and to deny them the right to vote in the first postwar elections. Commonwealth President Osme□a, however, countered that each case should be tried on its own merits. The successful Liberal Party presidential candidate, Manual Roxas, was among those collaborationists. Independence from the United States came on July 4, 1946, and Roxas was sworn in as the first president. The economy remained highly dependent on U.S. markets, and the United States also continued to maintain control of 23 military installations. A bilateral treaty was signed in March 1947 by which the United States continued to provide military aid, training, and matériel. Such aid was timely, as the Huk guerrillas rose again, this time against the new government. They changed their name to the People's Liberation Army (Hukbong Mapagpalaya ng Bayan) and demanded political participation, disbandment of the military police, and a general amnesty. Negotiations failed, and a rebellion began in 1950 with communist support. The aim was to overthrow the government. The Huk movement dissipated into criminal activities by 1951, as the better-trained and -equipped Philippine armed forces and conciliatory government moves toward the peasants offset the effectiveness of the Huks.

Populist Ramón Magsaysay of the Nacionalista Party was elected president in 1953 and embarked on widespread reforms that benefited tenant farmers in the Christian north while exacerbating hostilities with the Muslim south. The remaining Huk leaders were captured or killed, and by 1954 the movement had waned. After Magsaysay's death in an airplane crash in 1957, he was succeeded by Vice President Carlos P. Garcia. Garcia was elected in his own right the same year, and he advanced the nationalist theme of "Filipinos First," reaching agreement with the United States to relinquish large areas of land no longer needed for military operations. In 1961 the Liberal Party candidate, Diosdado Macapagal, was elected president. Subsequent negotiations with the United States over base rights led to considerable anti-American feelings and demonstrations. Macapagal sought closer relations with his Southeast Asian neighbors and convened a summit with the leaders of Indonesia and Malaysia in the hope of developing a spirit of consensus, which did not emerge.

The Marcos Era: Nacionalista Party leader Ferdinand Marcos came to dominate the political scene for the next two decades, beginning with his election to the presidency in 1965. During his first term, Marcos initiated ambitious public works projects that improved the general quality of life while providing generous pork-barrel benefits for his friends. Marcos perceived that his promised land reform program would alienate the politically all-powerful landowner elite, and thus it was never forcefully implemented. He lobbied strenuously for economic and military aid from the United States while resisting significant involvement in the Second Indochina War (1954–75). In 1967 the Philippines became a founding member of the Association of Southeast Asian Nations (ASEAN). Marcos became the first president to be reelected (in 1969), but early in his second term economic growth slowed, optimism faded, and the crime rate increased. In addition, a new communist insurgency, this time—starting in 1968—led by the new Communist Party of the Philippines-Marxist-Leninist and its military arm, the New People's Army, was on the rise. In 1969 the Moro National Liberation Front was founded and conducted an insurgency in Muslim areas. Political violence blamed on leftists, but probably initiated by government agents provocateurs, led Marcos to suspend habeas corpus as a prelude to martial law.

Marcos declared martial law on September 21, 1972, and did not lift it until January 17, 1981. During this time, he called for self-sacrifice and an end to the old society. However, in the "New Society" Marcos's cronies and his wife, former movie actress Imelda Romualdez-Marcos, wilfully engaged in rampant corruption. With her husband's support, Imelda Marcos built her own power base. She became governor of Metropolitan Manila and minister of human settlements. The previously nonpolitical armed forces became highly politicized, with high-ranking positions being given to Marcos loyalists. In 1979 the United States reaffirmed Philippine sovereignty over U.S. military bases and continued to provide military and economic aid to the Marcos regime. When martial law was lifted in 1981 and a "New Republic" proclaimed, little had actually changed, and Marcos easily won reelection.

The beginning of the end of the Marcos era occurred when his chief political rival, Liberal Party leader Benigno "Ninoy" Aquino, who had been jailed by Marcos for eight years, was assassinated as he disembarked from an airplane at the Manila International Airport on August 21, 1983, following medical treatment in the United States. Marcos cronies were charged with this crime but were acquitted. Aquino, however, became a martyr and his murder the focus of popular indignation against a corrupt regime. The Catholic Church, a coalition of old political opposition groups, the business elite, the left wing, and even factions of the armed forces all began to exert pressure on the regime. There also was foreign pressure and, feeling confident with the support given by the Reagan White House, Marcos called a "snap" presidential election for February 7, 1986. When the Marcos-dominated National Assembly proclaimed Marcos the winner, Cardinal Jaime Sin and key military leaders (including Minister of Defense Juan Ponce Enrile and acting Chief of Staff of the Armed Forces Lieutenant General Fidel V. Ramos) rallied around the apparent majority vote winner, Aquino's widow, Corazon Cojuango Aquino. The People Power Movement—a popular uprising of priests, nuns, ordinary citizens, and children, supported by defecting military units—ousted Marcos on the day of his inauguration (February 25, 1986) and brought Aquino to power in an almost bloodless revolution.

The Aquino Years and Beyond: Corazon Aquino had wide popular support but no political organization. Her vice president, Salvador H. "Doy" Laurel, had an organization but little popular support. Enrile and Ramos also had large stakes in what they saw as a coalition government. The coalition unraveled quickly, and there were several attempts, including unsuccessful military coups, to oust Aquino. She survived her fractious term, however, and was succeeded in the 1992 election by Ramos, who had served loyally as chief of staff of the armed forces and secretary of national defense under Aquino.

President Ramos worked at coalition building and overcoming the divisiveness of the Aquino years. Mutinous right-wing soldiers, communist insurgents, and Muslim separatists were convinced to cease their armed activities against the government and were granted amnesty. In an act of reconciliation, Ramos allowed the remains of Ferdinand Marcos—he had died in exile in the United States in 1989—to be returned to the Philippines for burial in 1993. Efforts by supporters of Ramos to gain passage of an amendment that would allow him to run for a second term were met with large-scale protests supported by Cardinal Sin and Corazon Aquino, leading Ramos to declare he would not run again.

Joseph Estrada, who had served as Ramos's vice president and enjoyed widespread popularity, was elected president in 1998. Within a year, however, Estrada's popularity declined sharply amid allegations of cronyism and corruption and failure to remedy the problems of poverty. Once again, street rallies supported by Cardinal Sin and Corazon Aquino took place. Then, in 2000 Senate investigators accused Estrada of having accepted bribes from illegal gambling businesses. Following an abortive Senate impeachment trial, growing street protests, and the withdrawal of support by the armed forces, Estrada was forced out of office on January 20, 2001.

Vice President Gloria Macapagal-Arroyo (the daughter of the late President Diosdado Macapagal) was sworn in as Estrada's successor on the day of his departure. Her accession to power was further legitimated by the mid-term congressional and local elections, when her coalition later won an overwhelming victory, but the elections were fraught with allegations of coercion, fraud, and vote buying. Macapagal-Arroyo's initial term in office was marked by fractious coalition politics as well as a military mutiny in Manila in July 2003 that led her to declare a month-long nationwide state of rebellion, as a result of which charges were filed against more than 1,000 individuals. Macapagal-Arroyo had declared in December 2002 that she would not contest the May 2004 presidential election, but she reversed herself in October 2003 and decided to run. She was reelected and sworn in for her own six-year term as president on June 30, 2004. With this new mandate, she was able to move with greater assurance on the political and economic reform agenda that had stalled during her first term in office.

GEOGRAPHY

Click to Enlarge Image

Location: The Philippines comprises an archipelago of some 7,107 islands located off Southeast Asia, between the South China Sea on the west and the Philippine Sea on the east. The major islands are Luzon in the north, the Visayan Islands in the middle, and Mindanao in the south.

Size: The total area is about 300,000 square kilometers, including about 298,000 square kilometers of land and about 2,000 square kilometers of water. The Philippines stretches about 1,850 kilometers from Y'Ami Island in the north to Sibutu Island in the south and is about 1,000 kilometers at its widest point east to west. The bulk of the population lives on 11 of the 7,107 islands.

Land Boundaries: The Philippines has no land boundaries. Nearby neighbors are Taiwan to the north, Malaysia and Indonesia to the south, Vietnam to the west, and China to the northwest.

Disputed Territory: The Philippines, China, Taiwan, Malaysia, and Vietnam hold conflicting claims to portions of the South China Sea and the Spratly Islands, which are called the Kalayaan (Freedom) Islands in the Philippines. The Philippines also disputes Malaysia's claim to the state of Sabah.

Length of Coastline: Estimates of the total length of the coastline range from 17,500 kilometers (official Philippine figure) to 36,289 kilometers (U.S. figure).

Maritime Claims: The Philippines claims a territorial sea of up to 100 nautical miles from the nearest coastline, an area that includes the entire Sulu Sea and the northern part of the Celebes Sea. A presidential decree in 1978 announced additional baselines, which in effect extended the territorial sea to claim an area up to 285 nautical miles in breadth in the South China Sea west of Palawan Island. This area encompasses the Spratly Islands. The Philippines also claims its continental shelf to the depth of exploitation and an exclusive economic zone of 200 nautical miles from its baselines.

Topography: The Philippines consists of volcanic islands, including active volcanoes, with mostly mountainous interiors surrounded by flat lowlands and alluvial plains of varying widths along the coasts. The elevation ranges from sea level to the highest point of Mount Apo on Mindanao Island, at 2,954 meters above sea level.

Principal Rivers: The longest river is the Cagayan (Río Grande de Cagayan) on Luzon, about 350 kilometers in length. Other principal rivers on Luzon include the Abra, Bicol, Chico, and Pampanga. The Pasig River is only about 25 kilometers in length but serves as the main waterway, flowing between Laguna de Bay, the largest freshwater lake in the Philippines, through metropolitan Manila to Manila Bay. Principal rivers on Mindanao include the Mindanao

River (known as the Pulangi River in its upper reaches), and the Agusan. The St. Paul River on Palawan is an eight-kilometer-long underground river.

Climate: The Philippines has a tropical marine climate, with the northeast monsoon, which produces a cool, dry season from December to February, and the southwest monsoon, which brings rain and high temperatures from May to October. Between March and May, hot, dry weather prevails. Temperatures in Manila range from 21⁰ C to 32⁰ C, with an average annual temperature of 27⁰ C. Temperatures elsewhere in the Philippines have been recorded at more than 37⁰ C. The average monthly humidity ranges from 71 percent in March to 85 percent in September. Annual rainfall is heavy but varies widely throughout the Philippines, ranging from 965 millimeters in some sheltered valleys and the southern tip of the island of Mindanao to 5,000 millimeters along the mountainous east coasts of the islands of Luzon, Samar, and the northern tip of Mindanao. The Philippines lies astride the typhoon belt and experiences 15 to 20 typhoons a year from July through October, of which five or six may cause serious destruction and death.

Natural Resources: The major natural mineral resources include coal, cobalt, copper, chromite, gold, gypsum, iron, natural gas, nickel, petroleum, salt, silver, and sulfur. There are lesser deposits of bauxite, lead, mercury, molybdenum, and zinc. Other important resources are geothermal and hydroelectric power, fish, and timber.

Land Use: Out of a total land area of about 300,000 square kilometers, about 92,000 square kilometers are farmland, and about 72,000 square kilometers are forest land, including 65,000 square kilometers of public land and 7,000 square kilometers of privately owned land. Forest area fell steadily from 270,000 square kilometers in 1900 to 80,000 square kilometers in 1970 and to 54,000 square kilometers in 1985. Although forest area subsequently grew from its low in 1985 to its current level in 2004, deforestation is still a major problem. According to the agricultural census of 2002, the number of farms decreased from 4.6 million in 1991 to 4.5 million in 2002, and farm area declined during the same period, from about 100,000 square kilometers in 1991 to its current level.

Environmental Factors: The Philippines is prone to natural disasters, particularly typhoons, floods, landslides, volcanic eruptions, earthquakes, and tsunamis, lying as it does astride the typhoon belt, in the active volcanic region known as the "Pacific Ring of Fire," and in the geologically unstable region between the Pacific and Eurasian tectonic plates. The Philippines also suffers major human-caused environmental degradation aggravated by a high annual population growth rate, including loss of agricultural lands, deforestation, soil erosion, air and water pollution, improper disposal of solid and toxic wastes, loss of coral reefs, mismanagement and abuse of coastal resources, and overfishing.

Time Zone: The Philippines is in one time zone (Asia/Manila), 8 hours ahead of Greenwich Mean Time.

SOCIETY

Population: The total population of the Philippines was 76.5 million, evenly divided between males and females, at the last census in May 2000. The Philippine National Statistics Office estimated that the total population reached 85.2 million in 2005. The average annual population growth rate from 1998 to 2004 was 2.1 percent. There has been a continuing trend of internal migration from rural to urban areas since at least 1991. According to the 2000 census, 52 percent of the population lived in rural areas and 48 percent in urban areas, including about 12 percent who lived in the National Capital Region, or Metropolitan Manila. The Philippines has a negligible loss of population as a result of emigration, which was estimated at –1.5 migrants per 1,000 population in 2004.

Demography: As of 2005, 35 percent of the population was 0–14 years of age; 61 percent, 15–64; and 4 percent, 65 and older. According to 2004 data, the gender ratio for the rising generation was 104 males for every 100 females. The birthrate was 25.8 births per 1,000 population. The death rate was 5.5 deaths per 1,000 population. Infant mortality was 24.2 deaths per 1,000 live births. Life expectancy at birth was 66.7 years for males, 72.6 years for females, and 69.6 years overall. The fertility rate was 3.2 children born per woman.

Ethnic Groups: Christian Malays constitute 91.5 percent of the total population, Muslim Malays 4 percent, Chinese 1.5 percent, and others 3 percent.

Languages: The Philippines has two official languages, Filipino (or Pilipino) and English. Filipino has eight major dialects, in order of use: Tagalog, Cebuano, Ilocano, Hiligaynon or Ilonggo, Bicol, Waray, Pampango, and Pangasinense. Filipino, based on Tagalog, is related to Malay and Indonesian and is part of the Malayo-Polynesian subgroup of the Austronesian language family. Filipino is the common language used between speakers of different native languages, which are closely related but not mutually intelligible. English is used in government and as the medium of instruction in higher education.

Religion: About 83 percent of the population is Roman Catholic; 9 percent Protestant, including Presbyterian, Methodist, Philippine Independent Church, and Philippine Church of Christ; 5 percent Muslim; and 3 percent Buddhist and other. The constitution guarantees freedom of religion and separation of church and state. But Christianity predominates, and Muslims historically have been marginalized.

Education and Literacy: Six years of primary education are free and compulsory; the four-year secondary education program is free but not compulsory. According to the Department of Education, for the school year 2002–3 a total of 12.9 million students were enrolled in elementary education (about 97 percent of the school-age population), including 12 million in public schools run by local government and 910,000 in private schools. A total of 6 million students were enrolled in secondary education (about 66 percent of the school-age population), including about 4.8 million in public schools and 1.2 million in private schools. In addition, about 2.4 million students were enrolled in higher education. At the end of 2005, the simple literacy rate was estimated at 93.4 percent, while the functional literacy rate was 84.1 percent.

Health: In 2000 the Philippines had about 95,000 physicians, or about 1 per 800 people. In 2001 there were about 1,700 hospitals, of which about 40 percent were government run and 60 percent private, with a total of about 85,000 beds, or about one bed per 900 people. The leading causes of morbidity as of 2002 were diarrhea, bronchitis, pneumonia, influenza, hypertension, tuberculosis, heart disease, malaria, chicken pox, and measles. Cardiovascular diseases account for more than 25 percent of all deaths. According to official estimates, 1,965 cases of human immunodeficiency virus (HIV) were reported in 2003, of which 636 had developed acquired immune deficiency syndrome (AIDS). Other estimates state that there may have been as many as 9,400 people living with HIV/AIDS in 2001.

Expenditures on health in 2002 totaled about US$2.2 billion, or about 2.9 percent of gross domestic product (GDP). Government expenditures on health accounted for only about 15 percent of total health expenditures, 30 percent of per capita health expenditures, and about 0.9 percent of all government spending. Per capita health expenditures in 2002 totaled US$28, of which government spending accounted for US$8. Both total and per capita expenditures on health have continued to decline since at least 1990, leading to a decrease in the share of GDP attributable to health expenditures. The main cause of this decline has been the high population growth rate. The government share of total spending on health also has declined steadily, and with more people, there has been less to spend per person from both the government and private sectors.

Welfare: The Philippines' social security system was established in 1957 and is compulsory for all employees, public and private. Retirement is compulsory at age 65 but optional at 60. An employees' compensation program, added in 1975, pays double compensation for work-related death, injury, or illness to employees who are not self-employed. The Philippine Health Insurance Corporation was established in 1995 to administer the National Health Insurance Program, with the stated goal of providing universal coverage. Annual premiums are about US$22. Retirees who have reached the age of 65, or who are older than 60 but not yet 65 and have already paid 120 monthly premiums, pay nothing. Depending on their level of income, heads of poorer households may pay the annual premium and have it include three other family members, as well as themselves. Indigents may have their entire premiums paid in part by the national government and in part by their local government. Benefits do not necessarily cover the full costs of medical expenses, and many poor people still cannot afford to pay the difference.

ECONOMY

Overview: The economy of the Philippines is an anomaly in the Asia-Pacific region in that it has lagged behind other economies, such as those of Singapore, South Korea, and Taiwan. From a position as one of the wealthiest countries in Asia after World War II, the Philippines is now one of the poorest. Since the 1970s, which were a relatively prosperous decade, the Philippines has failed to achieve a sustained period of rapid economic growth and has suffered from recurring economic crises. This persistent underperformance has occurred in spite of the Philippines' rich natural and human resources.

The reasons are rooted partly in history, partly in policy. As a legacy of the U.S. colonial period, oligopolies have dominated the economy, particularly in agriculture, where farmland continues to be concentrated in large estates. In the post-World War II period, the Philippines pursued a strategy of import substitution industrialization, whereby domestic goods are substituted for imports. This strategy required protectionist measures, which led to inefficiencies and the misallocation of resources. Although some trade protectionist measures were relaxed in the early twenty-first century, the Supreme Court continues to support restrictions on foreign ownership of land and other assets in effect since the constitution of 1935. These restrictions, plus widespread graft and corruption, have suppressed inbound foreign direct investment. A historically low rate of taxation—only about 15 percent of gross domestic product (GDP), partly as a result of widespread tax evasion—has led to underinvestment in infrastructure and uneven economic development.

The National Capital Region around Manila, which produces about 36 percent of GDP with only 12 percent of the population, is much more prosperous than rural areas, where much of the population depends on subsistence living. The traditional lack of job opportunities has led many Filipinos to seek employment outside the country, notably in the Persian Gulf states. Remittances to family members back home—equivalent to 10 percent of GDP—have partially offset a relatively low national rate of savings of about 15 to 18 percent, about average for the Organization for Economic Cooperation and Development, but below average for the region. Current account and budget deficits exacerbate the impact of the low savings rate on growth.

Although trade barriers were scaled back, industrial cartels split up, and limited reform measures taken in the late twentieth century, political instability, continuing high levels of corruption, and resistance to reforms by entrenched interests have prevented the Philippines from pursuing a consistent and effective economic course. The industrial sector continues to decline relative to services, an economic bright spot in which the Philippines apparently enjoys a comparative advantage, although some argue that services represent an employer of last resort. In 2005 the services sector accounted for about 53.5 percent of GDP; industry, 31.7 percent; and agriculture, forestry, and fishing, 14.8 percent.

Poverty is a serious problem in the Philippines. In 2003 per capita gross national income was US$1,080, below the US$1,390 average for lower-middle-income countries. Reflecting regional disparities, in 2003 about 11 percent of Filipinos lived on less than US$1 per day and 40 percent on less than US$2 per day, according to the World Bank. The overall poverty rate declined from 33 percent (25.4 million people) in 2000 to 30.4 percent (23.5 million people) in 2003. Poverty is more concentrated in rural than in urban areas.

Gross Domestic Product (GDP): In 2004 the gross domestic product (GDP) was US$84.6 billion, or US$1,150 on a per capita basis. According to purchasing power parity (PPP), however, GDP in 2005 was estimated to be US$451.3 billion, or US$5,100 per capita. In 2004 the Philippines achieved real economic growth of 6 percent, up from 4.5 percent in 2003. However, with the population expanding by more than 2 percent annually—one of the highest rates in Asia—the actual improvement in living standards is modest.

Government Budget: The budget has shown a deficit every year since 1998, but trends in the early twenty-first century are encouraging. In 2004 the deficit was US$3.4 billion, or about 3.9 percent of gross domestic product (GDP), conforming to the government's increasingly stringent targets for the second consecutive year. During 2005, the government expected to begin to close the revenue gap by introducing an expanded value-added tax. However, the tax's introduction was delayed pending resolution of a dispute over its constitutionality, which came on October 18 in a ruling by the Supreme Court. Historically, the persistent budget deficit, the result of overspending and poor collection by the Bureau of Internal Revenue, has placed restraints on economic growth.

Inflation: In 2005 consumer price inflation was 7.6 percent, up from 5.5 percent in 2004 and 3.0 percent in 2003. The rise in inflation reflected the combined impact of a depreciating peso, rising petroleum prices, and tariffs on electric power to offset losses at the state-owned power utility. The introduction of an expanded value-added tax is expected to provide an additional spur to inflation in 2006. Still, inflation remains well below the peak levels approaching 12 percent registered during the Asian financial crisis of 1997–98.

Agriculture, Forestry, and Fishing: The agricultural sector in the Philippines is known for low productivity, as it employs about 36 percent of the labor force but accounts for only 14.8 percent of gross domestic product (GDP). From 1991 to 2002, both the total number of farms and the total area of farmland decreased, respectively, from 4.6 million to 4.5 million farms and from 9.9 million hectares to 9.2 million hectares of farmland. The average size of each farm decreased from 2.2 hectares to 2.0 hectares.

In the first three quarters of 2005, crops accounted for 46.4 percent of the value of all agricultural production, livestock and poultry for 28.8 percent, and fishing for 24.9 percent. Overall agricultural production rose 1.7 percent over the same period in 2004. In order of value, major agricultural products were rice, poultry, livestock, corn, bananas, and coconuts. The national diet consists mainly of rice, fish, and vegetables, with occasional chicken and pork.

Forestry accounts for less than 1 percent of the total labor force and a minuscule share of all agricultural production, but at 72,000 square kilometers, it accounts for about 45 percent of all agricultural lands and about 25 percent of the total national land area. Once a major industry and the leading earner of foreign exchange in the 1960s, forestry has declined sharply in importance as a result of rapid deforestation. From a position as the world's leading exporter of tropical hardwoods in the 1970s, the Philippines became a net importer of forest products by the 1990s. In 1990 the Department of Environment and Natural Resources announced a 25-year plan for the sustainable development of the nation's forests. The Congress of the Philippines is considering a nationwide ban on logging; such bans already have been introduced in several provinces.

Fishing consists of municipal fishing, which uses no boats at all, rafts, or boats less than three tons; commercial fishing, which uses boats of three tons or more; and aquaculture farms. In 2004 municipal fishing accounted for about 34 percent of the value of all fishing production, 31 percent of the volume, and 85 percent of the fishing labor force. Commercial fishing accounted for 36 percent of the value, 32 percent of the volume, but only 1 percent of the fishing labor force. Aquaculture accounted for 30 percent of the value, 37 percent of the volume, and 14 percent of the fishing labor force.

Mining and Minerals: The Philippines has substantial copper, chromite, and gold deposits, and the country also is rich in many other minerals, including coal, cobalt, gypsum, iron, nickel, silver, and sulfur. There are also lesser deposits, not currently being mined, of bauxite, lead, mercury, molybdenum, and zinc. The latest exploration by the Minerals and Geosciences Bureau in 1996 estimated that the Philippines had 7.1 billion tons of metallic mineral reserves and 51 billion tons of nonmetallic mineral reserves. Of the metallic reserves, copper accounted for 4.8 billion tons, and gold accounted for 110,000 tons. Of the nonmetallic mineral reserves, limestone accounted for 29 billion tons and marble for 8.5 billion tons. The U.S. Department of State estimates that the Philippines possesses untapped mineral wealth of US$840 billion.

One of the world's top producers of chromite, copper, gold, and nickel in the 1970s and 1980s, the Philippines failed to rank in the top 10 worldwide for the production of any of these minerals or precious metals in 2002. With the closing of several major mines, mining has declined as a share of the gross domestic product (GDP) from a high of 30 percent in the industry's heyday to 1 percent in 2003. Aging infrastructure, high production costs, low commodity prices, and environmental concerns contributed to the decline. In 2003 mining employed only 4 percent of the labor force and claimed a negligible part, about 9,000 hectares, of the total land area.

However, the fortunes of the mining industry may be looking up. In 2003 President Gloria Macapagal-Arroyo announced that the government was shifting its policy from "tolerance to promotion of mining." Consistent with the president's policy, in December 2004 the Supreme Court issued a decision upholding the constitutionality of the 1995 Mining Act, which permits foreign companies to obtain mining and energy service contracts with the Philippine government. Following this decision, the local subsidiary of an Australian mining company announced a gold and copper mining service contract. The government hopes that additional foreign investment in the mining industry will be forthcoming.

Industry and Manufacturing: The production of consumer goods dominates the manufacturing sector. The leading industries are processed foods, followed by electrical machinery (mainly semiconductors), petroleum products, coal, chemical products, and garments. Industry accounted for about 32 percent and the manufacturing subsector for 23–24 percent of gross domestic product (GDP) in 2005. The number of persons employed in manufacturing and construction was about 16 percent of the total labor force in 2004.

Energy: In 2004 the Philippines derived 42 percent of its energy from oil; 30 percent from biomass, solar, and wind; 12 percent from coal; 7 percent from geothermal; 5 percent from hydropower; and 4 percent from natural gas. The Energy Development Plan for 2005–14 calls for the country to work toward energy independence by boosting domestic production of oil, gas, and coal and doubling the use of renewable sources of energy.

The Philippines has 152 million barrels of oil reserves and 3.7 trillion cubic feet of natural gas reserves. In 2004 the Philippines produced 25,000 barrels of oil per day, but domestic consumption was about 338,000 barrels per day, which meant that the Philippines was dependent on imports for about 92.5 percent of its needs. Consumption of oil has remained relatively stable so far this decade as the Philippines has met growing energy demand with electricity generated from natural gas produced by the Malampaya field in the South China Sea beginning in 2001. The Malampaya field, which has about 2.6 trillion cubic feet of natural gas reserves, produces about 25,000 barrels per day of natural gas. A deep-water pipeline carries natural gas to an onshore power station. Eventually, three such stations will have a combined capacity of 2,700 megawatts. In 2003 the Philippines consumed 9.6 million short tons of coal, of which 7.4 million tons (77 percent) were imported. The Philippines is the second largest producer of geothermal power in the world after the United States, and geothermal power accounts for about 50 percent of domestic power generation, followed by hydropower, which accounts for about 33 percent. The development of hydropower through the construction of large dams, however, has been controversial. Its proponents argue that the dams provide flood control, irrigation, and more self-sufficiency in energy. Its opponents argue that the dams destroy valuable natural habitat and displace thousands of local people without adequate compensation. Other power sources are natural gas, coal, and oil. There are no operational nuclear power plants in the Philippines. The Bataan Nuclear Power Plant, completed in 1985, had its operations suspended in 1986 because of corruption charges, and in 1997 the government decided to convert the idle plant to a natural gas power plant. The Philippines continues to pursue the privatization of the state-owed National Power Company known as Napocor, but so far the initiative has been plagued by delays. Possible reasons include poor infrastructure and inflated valuations.

Services: The services sector, in which the Philippines apparently enjoys a comparative advantage, has grown steadily since 1985, when it accounted for about 40 percent of both gross domestic product (GDP) and the total number of persons employed. By 1999, services accounted for about 52 percent of GDP and about 45 percent of the total number of persons employed, and by 2004 those figures had risen to 53 percent and 48 percent, respectively. In the first half of 2005, the services sector grew more quickly (by 6.6. percent) than industry or agriculture. The fastest growing segments of the services sector were telecommunications, business outsourcing, and financial services.

Banking and Finance: The Central Bank of the Philippines supervises the nation's banking system. Nonbank financial intermediaries such as private insurance companies are overseen by the Insurance Commission and the Securities and Exchange Commission. The largest domestic banks, in order of size, are Metropolitan Bank and Trust (Metrobank), Bank of the Philippine Islands, Equitable-PCI Banking Corporation, Land Bank of the Philippines, Philippine National Bank, Development Bank of the Philippines, Rizal Commercial Banking Corporation, Banco de Oro, Allied Banking Corporation, and China Banking Corporation. There also are 32 other universal and commercial banks. Four of the banks are owned or controlled by the government: the Land Bank of the Philippines, the Philippine National Bank, the Development Bank of the Philippines, and the Al-Amanah Islamic Bank. In addition, the banking sector includes 93 thrift banks (savings and mortgage banks, stock savings and loan associations, private development banks, and micro-finance institutions) and 771 rural banks. The universal and commercial banks and the largest thrift banks have licences to operate foreign-currency deposit units. Foreign banks provide competition to local banks and are active in investment banking, asset management, and foreign-exchange and derivatives trading. Although they have a small market share and branch networks are not extensive, the expertise and reputation of the foreign banks attract customers.

The banking sector was relatively undamaged by the Asian financial crisis of 1997–98, and since 2001 asset quality has improved. In July 2005, nonperforming loans declined into the single digits (9.3 percent), half the peak level (18.8 percent) recorded in October 2001. This progress reflects the positive impact of the Special Purpose Vehicle Act of 2002, which provided incentives to financial institutions to reduce non-performing assets. Another trend in commercial banking is toward consolidation and restructuring.

The capitalization of the stock market is still modest, but it is growing rapidly off a low base. At the end of 2005, total stock market capitalization reached US$113 billion, up 25 percent from the previous year. During 2005, initial public offerings reached their highest level since the Asian financial crisis in 1997–98: US$1.06 billion. However, fewer than 1 percent of Filipinos invest in the stock market. Filipino investors generally prefer the bond market, which they regard as safer, and foreign investors also lack confidence in the stock market. The most important index, the Philippine Composite Index (PHISIX), consists of 34 listed issues, representing the country's most important companies. The main financial centers are in Manila, the location of the Philippine Stock Exchange, and in Cebu.

The Philippines had 34 life insurance firms in 2005; this number includes foreign insurers that dominate the industry. Three foreign-owned life insurers and four joint-venture (foreign and domestic) life insurers enjoyed a combined market share of about 60 percent. The Philippine American Life Insurance Company is the largest life insurance issuer with a market share of 23.6 percent.

Tourism: In 2005 about 2.6 million foreign tourists visited the Philippines—a record high. Tourists came from the following regions, listed in order of volume: East Asia, North America, Association of South East Asian Nations, and Australiasia/Pacific. Authorities were hopeful that visitors could reach 3 million in 2006. Tourism has grown significantly since the first three years of the decade, when about 1.9 million foreigners visited the country each year. The Department of Tourism has actively promoted tourism to take advantage of the fact that the indirect impact of tourism on the economy is 2.5 times the actual money spent by visitors, according to a study by economists at the University of Asia and the Pacific. Prior to 2005, tourism had failed to flourish as a result of political and economic instability, the terrorist threat in the southern provinces, and the perception that other countries in the region offer better attractions. The Philippines is seeking more investment in hotels, restaurants, and other tourism-related infrastructure.

Labor: In December 2005, the unemployment rate was 7.4 percent, much lower than the roughly 11 percent average typical since the mid-1980s. The improvement was attributable to electronics exports, the end of drought conditions for agriculture, and growth in business outsourcing, real estate, and tourism. Some 32.9 million people were employed out of a total workforce of 35.5 million. However, the underemployment rate was 21.2 percent. In 2004 about 48 percent were employed in services, 36 percent in agriculture, and 16 percent in industry. Reflecting the lack of satisfactory employment opportunities at home, an estimated 652,000 Filipinos obtained employment outside the country as contract workers. About 4 million workers belong to trade unions, which are particularly prevalent in manufacturing. Labor relations generally are good because of the strict enforcement of labor laws and the acceptance of collective bargaining.

However, in 2003 some 38 new strikes, mostly attributable to unfair labor practices, led to the loss of 156,000 workdays, less than half the level in the previous year.

Foreign Economic Relations: The Philippines' foreign economic relations revolve around its Asian neighbors, with which it conducts a majority of its trade, and the United States, which is a major trading partner. The Philippines helped to found the Association of Southeast Asian Nations (ASEAN) in 1967. The Philippines also belongs to the Asia-Pacific Economic Cooperation (APEC) forum. ASEAN's goal of establishing a regional free-trade area has been only partially realized.

The Philippines has been a member of the World Trade Organization (WTO) since January 1, 1995. In 2001 the Philippine Bureau of International Trade Relations issued a positive assessment of the WTO's impact on the country's economic development. WTO membership has enabled the Philippines to adopt transparent trade rules regarding customs valuation, defenses against unfair trade, and protection of intellectual property rights. For example, in 1998 the government passed a law that improves the protection of intellectual property rights in the areas of copyrights, patents, and trademarks. However, the United States maintains that the intellectual property protections are inadequate and has taken initial steps toward imposing trade sanctions.

Imports: In 2004 the Philippines' imports were valued at US$45.1 billion, up 10.6 percent from the previous year. Principal imports were telecommunications and electronics equipment (34 percent), chemicals (7 percent), and crude petroleum (6 percent). The main origins of imports were Japan (19.8 percent), the United States (13.7 percent), China (7.7 percent), Singapore (7.4 percent), Taiwan (7.0 percent), and South Korea (5.6 percent).

Exports: In 2004 the Philippines' exports were valued at US$38.7 billion, up 9.6 percent from the previous year. Principal exports were electronic products (68.8 percent), clothing (5.6 percent), coconut oil (1.5 percent), and petroleum products (1.0 percent). Exported electronic products were primarily semiconductors. The main destinations of exports were Japan (20.1 percent), the United States (17.9 percent), the Netherlands (9.1 percent), Hong Kong (7.9 percent), China (6.7 percent), and Singapore (6.6 percent).

Trade Balance: In 2004 the Philippines incurred a merchandise trade deficit of US$6.4 billion, or 14 percent of imports. However, remittances of US$8.8 billion from Filipinos working overseas during 2004 more than offset the trade deficit. Such remittances surpassed US$10.8 billion in 2005. As recently as 2002, the Philippines had a slight trade surplus.

Balance of Payments: In 2004 the current account balance was US$2.1 billion. Since 1998, the Philippines has achieved a positive current account balance. Reflecting the sustained period of balance of payments surpluses, gross international reserves rose to a record US$18.6 billion in September 2005.

External Debt: In 2004 external debt amounted to US$61 billion, or 72.2 percent of gross domestic product (GDP).

Foreign Investment: In 2004 direct investment inflows were a modest US$57 million. Over the long term, direct and portfolio investment have been anemic, reflecting the relative unattractiveness of the economy, restrictions on foreign ownership, and the perception of political risk. The three top sources of foreign direct investment—ranked by amount—are the United States, Japan, and the Netherlands.

Currency and Exchange Rate: The currency is the Philippine peso (PHP). In mid-March 2006, the exchange rate was approximately PHP51 = US$1. The peso is made up of 100 centavos. Coins are issued in denominations of 1, 5, 10, and 25 centavos and 1, 5, and 10 pesos. Banknotes are issued in denominations ranging from 5 pesos to 1,000 pesos.

Fiscal Year: Calendar year.

TRANSPORTATION AND TELECOMMUNICATIONS

Overview: The transportation system faces the fundamental geographic challenge that the Philippines is a far-flung archipelago. This fact offers a partial explanation for the country's relatively undeveloped transportation infrastructure. Another reason is the sustained underinvestment in infrastructure since the 1997–98 Asian economic crisis. In 2003, for example, infrastructure investment accounted for only 3.6 percent of gross domestic product, well below the rate of investment in Thailand (15.4 percent) and Vietnam (9.9 percent). Consequently, the Philippines ranked 89 out of 102 countries in infrastructure quality in 2004, according to the World Economic Forum. Among developing economies in East Asia, the Philippines ranked last for the quality of its railroads, ports, and electrical systems. The road network is mostly unpaved, only slightly more than half of the limited railroad system is in operation, and only a few ports have major passenger and cargo terminals. President Gloria Macapagal-Arroyo hopes to establish a highway and ferry network that will ease travel across the archipelago.

Roads: Although an extensive road network covers almost the entire nation, the quality varies widely, and traffic congestion is common, particularly in Manila. Local governments are responsible for managing some 86 percent of the 202,000-kilometer network. An estimated 60 percent of roads are unpaved village roads. As for the national network, 70.4 percent of roads are paved with concrete or asphalt, with the remainder consisting of gravel or earth. In urban areas, transportation is available by car, bus, light rail, metro rail, and jeepney. The highly decorated but popular jeepney, a derivative of the World War II-era U.S. Army jeep, has been adapted to public transportation. In the provinces, buses, jeepneys, and three-wheeled taxis are the main modes of ground transportation. A priority in the nation's lagging road investment program is the improvement of roads carrying goods to and from ports.

Railroads: The Philippines has 897 kilometers of railroads, but much of the network in the north is closed because of its poor condition. The main railroad line, of which 440 kilometers are operational, is located on the island of Luzon, the largest island in the archipelago and home of Manila. On Luzon, the Philippine National Railways provides long-distance service, while in Metropolitan Manila, the Metro Rail Transit Authority and Light Rail Transit Authority provide elevated, light-rail service.

Ports: As an archipelago, the Philippines has more than 1,000 ports, of which 117 are regarded as international ports. The Philippines Port Authority, which administers the ports, has the mission of promoting maritime trade within the context of the Philippines' hoped-for transformation into a newly industrialized country. About 12 of the 117 international ports have major cargo and passenger terminals. The premier cargo terminal is in the Port of Manila. The domestic ports service inter-island boats, ferries, and roll-on, roll-off vessels. Some remote islands are accessible only by boat. In 2003 privately controlled ports accounted for 54 percent of total cargo serviced. Private ports generally handle more international trade, whereas government-run ports service mainly domestic trade.

Inland Waterways: The Philippines has 3,219 kilometers of inland waterways. The nation's inland waterway system is the thirty-second largest in the world.

Civil Aviation/Airports: The Philippines has 87 airports, including four major international airports: Mactan-Cebu International on Mactan Island in Cebu province, Ninoy Aquino International in Manila, Diosdado Macapagal International at the former U.S. Air Force base at Clark Field, north of Manila, and Davao International Airport near Davao City on Mindanao. Most of the other regional airports are substandard. The government is working on improving the civil aviation infrastructure. A legal dispute is holding up the opening of a newly constructed terminal at Ninoy Aquino International Airport. A consortium of international companies is seeking to recover investments in the project, following the revocation of the group's build-operate-transfer contract and seizure of the terminal by President Macapagal-Arroyo's administration. The government plans to complete the terminal in early 2006, but the opening is likely to be delayed. The flagship airline is Philippine Airlines, which serves 32 foreign and 21 domestic cities with a fleet of 30 Boeing and Airbus aircraft.

Pipelines: In October 2001, multinational energy companies began to tap natural gas from the Malampaya offshore field in the South China Sea by completing a 502-kilometer pipeline, one of the longest deep-water pipelines in the world. The Malampaya field is believed to contain 2.6 trillion cubic feet of natural gas. The natural gas will be used to fuel three power plants with a combined annual capacity of 2,700 megawatts.

Telecommunications: Mobile telecommunications are more popular than fixed-line telecommunications in the Philippines. An estimated 30–40 million Filipinos have cell phones. The Philippines uses the Global System for Mobile Communications, a second-generation digital technology employed by 71 percent of the world market. In November 2004, the National Telecommunications Commission held initial hearings to lay the groundwork for the introduction of third-generation digital technology, already widely used in the United States, Europe, and much of the Asia-Pacific region. In December 2005, the government authorized four domestic carriers to provide third-generation cellular service beginning in 2008. Third-generation technology enables high-speed, high-bandwidth video applications by cell phone. Currently, Short Message Service, a system for text messages under 160 characters in length, is widely used, with more than 200 million messages transmitted per day, but Multimedia Message Service has been gaining acceptance since its introduction in 2003.

In 2003 the Philippines had 11.5 million radios, 3.7 million televisions, and 1.5 million personal computers. Internet access is modest, particularly in comparison to other countries in the region. Whereas South Korea boasts the world's highest Internet broadband penetration rate, only about 5 million Filipinos have Internet access, and 85 percent of them rely on dial-up connections. The Philippine Long Distance Company, the largest telecommunications provider, is responsible for maintaining a national digital fiber-optic network, digital microwave radio, and satellite communications.

GOVERNMENT AND POLITICS

Overview: In February 1987, the Philippines adopted a new constitution that instituted the presidential-style republican form of democracy, which resembles the U.S. model much more than the European parliamentary system. One key difference between the Philippine and U.S. systems is that the Philippines is a unitary republic, whereas the United States is a federal republic, with significant powers reserved for the states. In the Philippines, by contrast, the national government is not challenged by local authority. The ratification of the 1987 constitution—the fourth in the nation's history—by national referendum signaled the country's return to democracy following the autocratic rule of Fernando Marcos (1965–86). Politics in the Philippines is somewhat tumultuous. In February 2006, the president declared a state of emergency after quashing the attempted coup staged by the political opposition.

Executive Branch: Embracing the concept of separation of powers, the constitution provides for a president, who is simultaneously head of government and chief of state, a separately elected vice president, a bicameral legislature, and an independent judiciary. The constitution includes legislative and judicial limits on the power of the president. The president cannot abolish Congress, and Congress can override a presidential veto with a two-thirds majority vote. Moreover, the president needs Congressional support in order to implement policies and programs. The Supreme Court rules on the constitutionality of presidential decrees.

The president is elected to a single six-year term by direct universal suffrage; the vice president may be elected to a maximum of two consecutive six-year terms. The vice president may be appointed to the cabinet without legislative confirmation. The current president is Gloria Macapagal-Arroyo, who originally took office in January 2001, when she succeeded Joseph Estrada following his impeachment in November 2000. In May 2004, Macapagal-Arroyo was elected to a full term. The vice president, since June 2004, is Noli de Castro. The executive functions of the government are carried out through the Cabinet of Ministers. The cabinet, which in 2005 consisted of heads of 22 departments and offices, is appointed by the president with the consent of the Commission of Appointments.

Legislative Branch: The bicameral Congress of the Philippines consists of the Senate (upper chamber) and House of Representatives (lower chamber). Members of the 24-seat Senate are elected at large to six-year terms and are limited to no more than two consecutive terms. The current president of the Senate (since 2000) is Franklin M. Drilon. The House is limited by the constitution to no more than 250 members. In 2005 there were 238 members, of whom 214 (80 percent) were elected for three-year terms from legislative districts apportioned among the provinces, cities, and the Metropolitan Manila area in accordance with the population, on the basis of a uniform and progressive ratio. The other 24 members (limited by the constitution to 20 percent of the total) are presidential appointees elected through a party-list system of registered national, regional, and sectoral parties or organizations. House members are limited to no more than three consecutive terms. The current speaker of the House (now in his third term as speaker, most recently since 2004) is José de Venecia. By means of a two-thirds majority vote, Congress can override presidential vetoes and declare a state of war.

Judicial Branch: The Philippines has an independent judiciary, with the Supreme Court as the highest court of appeal. The Supreme Court also is empowered to review the constitutionality of presidential decrees. The Supreme Court consists of a chief justice and 14 associate justices. It is not necessary for the entire court to convene in all cases. Justices are appointed by the president on the recommendation of the Judicial and Bar Council and serve until 70 years of age. The current chief justice, since 1998, is Hilario G. Davide, Jr. Lower-level courts include a national Court of Appeals divided into 17 divisions, local and regional trial courts, and an informal local system to settle certain disputes outside the formal court system. In 1985 a separate court system founded on Islamic law (sharia) was established in the southern Philippines with jurisdiction over family and contractual relations among Muslims. Three district magistrates and six circuit judges oversee the Islamic law system. A special court—the Sandiganbayan or anti-graft court— focuses exclusively on investigating charges of judicial corruption.

Administrative Divisions: Administrative divisions consist of regions, provinces, chartered cities, municipalities, and *barangays* (villages). Chartered cities are not part of any province and do not elect provincial officials. The Philippines has 17 regions, 79 provinces, 117 chartered cities, 1,500 municipalities, and 41,975 *barangays*. Metropolitan Manila, which is regarded as a region, consists of 14 cities, 3 municipalities, and 1,694 *barangays*. The Autonomous Region in Muslim Mindanao was established in 1990 following a plebicite in late 1989.

Provincial and Local Government: Governors and vice governors are elected to head provinces, the largest local administrative unit. Appointed functionaries responsible for managing offices concerned with finance, tax collection, audit, public works, agricultural services, health, and schools are subordinate not just to the governor, but also to national ministries. Because the Philippines is a unitary republic, local government has less power than it would have in a federal system. In fact, according to the constitution, the president oversees local government. The single biggest problem for local government has been inadequate funding. Although local government is permitted to levy taxes, such taxes are subject to restrictions by Congress, and they have been difficult to collect in practice. A fragmented four-province Autonomous Region in Muslim Mindanao was formally established in November 1990 with its own governor and unicameral legislature.

Judicial and Legal System: The basis of the legal code is primarily Spanish and Anglo-American law. Islamic law applies among Muslims in portions of the southern Philippines. According to the constitution, those accused of crimes have the right to be informed of the charges against them, to be represented by counsel, and to have a speedy and fair public trial. Defendants also enjoy the presumption of innocence and have the right to confront witnesses, present evidence, and appeal convictions. However, the judiciary is said to suffer from corruption and inefficiency, which at times undermine the provision of due process and equal justice. As a result, the Supreme Court has undertaken a five-year program to speed up the judicial process and crack down on corruption.

Electoral System: The Philippines has universal direct suffrage at age 18 and older to elect the president, vice president (who runs independently), and most of the seats in the bicameral legislature, consisting of the House of Representatives and the Senate; a minority of House members known as sectoral representatives are appointed by the president. Elections are held not just for national leadership but also for representation at the provincial and local levels. In the last elections in May 2004, some 74 percent of eligible voters participated, but the process was marred by violence and numerous irregularities, which the political opposition continues to protest, even calling for the president's impeachment.

Politics and Political Parties: President Macapagal-Arroyo represents the conservative Lakas-Christian Muslim Democratic Party (Lakas-CMD), since the May 2004 election the largest faction in the House of Representatives (100 seats). Lakas-CMD has formed a governing coalition with the Liberal Party (32 seats). Others parties in the House are the Nationalist Peoples Coalition (47 seats); Struggle for Democratic Filipinos (nine seats); Nationalista Party (six seats); Akbayan (three seats); Association of Philippine Electric Co-operatives (three seats); Bayan Muna (three seats); Power of the Filipino Masses (three seats); Aksyon Demokratiko, Promdi, and Reporma, which have formed an alliance (two seats); Philippine Democratic Party (two seats); and Philippines Democratic Socialist Party (two seats). Personalities are more important than parties in Philippine politics. Movie stars and other celebrities have enjoyed considerable success. In addition, several prominent families play a disproportionate role in politics.

Mass Media: The Office of the President is responsible for managing the government's policy toward the press, but freedom of speech and freedom of the press are enshrined in the 1987 constitution. Although independent observers credit the government with respecting freedom of the press in general, the government has been criticized for failing to investigate thoroughly summary killings of journalists and for subjecting journalists to harassment and surveillance. The most widely read newspapers are the *Manila Bulletin, Philippine Star, Philippine Daily Inquirer, Manila Times,* and *Business World.* In 2004 the country had 225 television stations, 369 AM radio broadcast stations, 583 FM radio broadcast stations, and 5 shortwave stations. Although some media outlets, such as IBC (television) and the Philippine Broadcasting Service (radio), are government-run, most outlets are privately owned. Much media ownership is concentrated in the hands of prominent families and businesses. Consequently, some reports tend to be one-sided presentations favoring special interests. The privately owned press also tends toward sensationalism at times.

Foreign Relations: The foreign policy of the Philippines aims to promote democracy and human rights and the welfare of some 7 million overseas workers. The Philippines maintains close ties to Persian Gulf and other Middle Eastern nations where many of these workers are employed. In an effort to expand its relationship with the Islamic world, the Philippines is seeking observer status in the Organization of the Islamic Conference. The Philippines is an active member of the Association of Southeast Asian Nations. The Philippines also has participated in a variety of United Nations-sponsored peacekeeping missions. However, in July 2004, after a Filipino truck driver was taken hostage in Iraq, the Philippines elected to withdraw troops from that embattled nation in order to win his release.

The Philippines maintains strong ties to the United States, which designated the nation a major non-North Atlantic Treaty Organization ally in 2003. Although the United States mildly rebuked the Philippines for yielding to insurgent demands in Iraq to withdraw its small contingent, the United States continues to view the Philippines as an important ally in the war on terrorism, particularly in view of various Islamic insurgencies on the islands of Mindanao and Jolo. The relationship with the United States was redefined in the early 1990s, when the United States complied with Philippine demands to vacate various military bases, including the naval base at Subic Bay. However, the two nations remain close, and in May 2004 the Philippines signed an agreement with the United States exempting U.S. military personnel in the Philippines from prosecution before the International Criminal Court.

The Philippines has an improving, but still fragile, relationship with China. As reflected in President Macapagal-Arroyo's visit to China in 2001, the Philippines is seeking closer economic cooperation with China, even as it fears China's growing economic and military clout. A territorial dispute over control of the Spratly Islands in the South China Sea is an impediment to better relations. China also is concerned about the Philippines' strong ties to the United States, which it views as a strategic rival in the region.

The Philippines cooperates with the neighboring countries of Indonesia and Malaysia in combating the regional threat posed by the Islamic terrorist group Jemaah Islamiyah. Relations with Indonesia improved following the ouster of President Suharto in May 1998 after 32 years of authoritarian rule. Suharto's overthrow mirrored Ferdinand Marcos's overthrow in the Philippines in 1986. The Philippines' relations with Malaysia are somewhat impaired by a territorial dispute over the state of Sabah, which is now part of Malaysia.

Japan and the United States are the Philippines' leading trading partners and sources of direct investment. Japan is the top source of development assistance. Australia also is a significant economic and security partner. The Philippines and Singapore share a close economic and political relationship with the United States, and the two nations have engaged in joint military training exercises.

Membership in International Organizations: The Philippines belongs to the United Nations (UN), the World Trade Organization, and several key Asian regional organizations, notably the Association of Southeast Asian Nations (ASEAN), ASEAN's Regional Forum, the Asian Development Bank, and the Asia Pacific Economic Cooperation (APEC) forum. In addition, the Philippines is a member of the following international organizations: Colombo Plan, Customs Cooperation Council, Group of 24, Group of 77, International Chamber of Commerce, International Confederation of Free Trade Unions, International Criminal Police Organization, International Federation of Red Cross and Red Crescent Societies, International Hydrographic Organization, International Olympic Committee, International Organization for Migration, International Organization for Standardization, Non-Aligned Movement, Organisation for the Prohibition of Chemical Weapons, World Confederation of Labor, World Federation of Trade

Unions, and World Tourism Organization. The Philippines has applied for observer status in the Organization of the Islamic Conference.

During 2004–5 the Philippines served as a temporary member of the UN Security Council. The Philippines is a permanent member of the following UN-affiliated organizations: Economic and Social Commission for Asia and the Pacific, Food and Agriculture Organization, International Atomic Energy Agency, International Bank for Reconstruction and Development (World Bank), International Civil Aviation Organization, International Development Association, International Finance Corporation, International Fund for Agricultural Development, International Labour Organization, International Maritime Organization, International Monetary Fund, International Telecommunication Union, UN Conference on Aid and Development, UN Educational, Scientific and Cultural Organization, UN Industrial Development Organization, UN Office of the High Commissioner for Refugees, UN University, Universal Postal Union, World Health Organization, World Intellectual Property Organization, and World Meteorological Organization.

Major International Treaties: The Philippines is a party to the following environmental agreements: Biodiversity, Climate Change, Climate Change-Kyoto Protocol, Desertification, Endangered Species, Hazardous Wastes, Law of the Sea, Marine Dumping, Ozone Layer Protection, Ship Pollution, Tropical Timber 83, Tropical Timber 94, Wetlands, and Whaling. The Philippines has signed, but not ratified, the agreement on Air Pollution-Persistent Organic Pollutants. In the area of arms control, the Philippines is a party to the Biological Weapons Convention, Chemical Weapons Convention, Treaty on the Non-Proliferation of Nuclear Weapons, and Limited Test Ban Treaty. The Philippines has ratified numerous international human rights agreements, including those against slavery, genocide, prisoner of war abuse, human trafficking, racial discrimination, and torture. The Philippines also has adopted agreements designed to protect women, children, and refugees. Although the Philippines is a member of the World Intellectual Property Organization (WIPO), it has not ratified the WIPO Performances and Phonograms Treaty or the Copyright Treaty.

NATIONAL SECURITY

Armed Forces Overview: The Armed Forces of the Philippines (AFP) consists of a 66,000-member army; a 24,000-member navy, including 7,500 marines; and a 16,000-member air force. Active forces are supplemented by 131,000 reserves. A joint service command covers five military areas. The 6,000-member National Capital Region Command, established in November 2003, is responsible for protecting the government against coup attempts. The president of the republic is commander in chief of the armed forces. The AFP is poorly funded and is armed with antiquated equipment. In 2003 the government moved to replace World War II-era rifles. In addition, only slightly more than half of the Philippines' naval ships are operational, and only a few air force planes are combat ready. Compounding the problem of inadequate equipment, the AFP's leadership has been accused of corruption and complicity with insurgent groups, although its primary mission involves counterinsurgency. In July 2003, junior officers staged an unsuccessful coup. The Philippines is the recipient of U.S. military assistance.

Foreign Military Relations: The United States and the Philippines have a mutual defense treaty that has been in effect since 1952, but it does not extend to territorial disputes involving the Spratly Islands. In 2003 the United States designated the Philippines as a major non-North Atlantic Treaty Organization ally. Total U.S. military assistance to the Philippines rose from US$38 million in 2001 to US$114 million in 2003 and a projected US$164 million in 2005, which would make the Philippines the fourth largest recipient of U.S. foreign military assistance. Australia reportedly also a major source of military assistance.

External Threat: The Philippines faces no major external threat.

Defense Budget: The defense budget for 2005 totaled US$840 million, or 5 percent of the proposed government budget of US$16.5 billion. Almost half of the defense budget was designated for the army. Viewed another way, 80 percent of the budget was slated for personnel and almost the entire remaining amount, for maintenance and operating expenses. Thus, less than 1 percent was available for desperately needed procurement.

Major Military Units: The army has eight light infantry divisions, one special operations command, five engineering battalions, one artillery regiment at headquarters, one presidential security group, and three light-reaction companies. The navy has two commands—Fleet and Marine Corps. Navy bases are located at Sangley Point/Cavite, Zamboanga, and Cebu. The air force is organized into headquarters and five commands: air defense, tactical operations, air education and training, air logistics and supply, and air reserves.

Major Military Equipment: The army is equipped with 65 light tanks, 85 armored infantry fighting vehicles, and 370 armored personnel carriers, as well as towed artillery, mortars, recoilless launchers, and several small aircraft. The navy is equipped with one frigate; 58 patrol and coastal combatants; 7 amphibious ships, plus about 39 amphibious craft; and 11 support and miscellaneous vessels. However, in April 2003 the armed forces chief of staff stated that only 56 percent of the navy's vessels were operational. Naval aviation has six transport aircraft and four search-and-rescue helicopters. The air force has 36 combat aircraft and 25 armed helicopters.

Military Service: The Armed Forces of the Philippines (AFP) is an all-volunteer force. The minimum age for service is 20 years.

Paramilitary Forces: Paramilitary forces include the civilian Philippine National Police (under the Department of Interior and Local Government), with an estimated 115,000 personnel; the Coast Guard (run by the navy but technically part of the Department of Transportation and Communications), numbering 3,500; and local citizen armed militias, the Civilian Armed Forces Geographical Units (CAFGUs) estimated to number 40,000–82,000.

Foreign Military Forces: Beginning in 2002, the U.S. military has assisted the Armed Forces of the Philippines in fighting the Abu Sayyaf Group (ASG), an al Qaeda affiliate. Although foreign militaries are formally banned from conducting operations on Philippine soil, the U.S. military has maintained an officially advisory presence in the Philippines continuously since 2002. The two nations regularly conduct joint training exercises in the Philippines.

Military Forces Abroad: The Philippines has participated in a variety of United Nations (UN)-sponsored peacekeeping missions, most recently the UN Mission in Burundi, the UN Mission of Support in East Timor, the UN Stabilization Mission in Haiti, the UN Mission in Ivory Coast, and the UN Mission in Liberia. The Philippines also participated in United States-led operations in Iraq, with troops involved in humanitarian assistance starting in August 2003. However, the Philippines decided to withdraw its small force in July 2004 when insurgents took a Filipino truck driver hostage.

Police: The Department of Interior and Local Government oversees the Philippine National Police (PNP), which has an active force of about 115,000. The PNP, which had been entrusted with internal security in 1996, lost this role two years later, when the Armed Forces of the Philippines—particularly the army—reasserted its lead role in internal security. In September 2002, the PNP regained some of its authority when it was allowed to form a counterinsurgency task force in northeast Mindanao. Meanwhile, the army established a parallel task force in southwest Mindanao.

Internal Threat: Insurgencies by various Islamic terrorist and separatist groups and the communist New People's Army pose a significant internal threat. In response to this situation and the global war on terrorism, the Armed Forces of the Philippines (AFP) has been restructured to combat domestic insurgencies, most of which are based on the southern island of Mindanao: the Moro Islamic Liberation Front (MILF), the Abu Sayyaf Group (ASG), Jemaah Islamiyah, and the Communist Party of the Philippines' New People's Army (NPA). In addition, the loyalty of the military to the government remains in doubt, following an unsuccessful coup by a renegade faction of the AFP in July 2003.

Terrorism: The Philippines faces an indigenous terrorist threat from several organizations: the Moro Islamic Liberation Front (MILF), the Abu Sayyaf Group (ASG), Jemaah Islamiyah (JI), and the communist New People's Army (NPA). The MILF and ASG, which aspire to establish an Islamic state on Mindanao, are reputed to have links to al Qaeda. The MILF, which has engaged in sporadic peace negotiations with the government and has some moderate elements, is the largest of the groups, with about 10,000 to 11,000 soldiers. The more militant ASG, after being forced to abandon its stronghold on the island of Basilan by the Armed Forces of the Philippines, has regrouped on Jolo. About 400 guerrillas now are affiliated with the group, about half the original level before its confrontation with the Philippine military. Jemaah Islamiyah, an al Qaeda affiliate active in Indonesia but with branches across Southeast Asia, allegedly failed to execute plans to bomb ceremonies marking the inauguration of the new Philippine government in June 2004. The NPA, the military wing of the Communist Party of the Philippines, has about 3,000 guerrillas on Mindanao.

Human Rights: According to a U.S. Department of State report released in March 2006, Philippine security forces have been responsible for serious human rights abuses despite the efforts of civilian authorities to control them. The report found that although the government generally respected human rights, some security forces elements—particularly the Philippine National Police—practiced extrajudicial killings, vigilantism, disappearances, torture, and arbitrary arrest and detention in their battle against criminals and terrorists. Prison conditions were harsh, and the slow judicial process as well as corrupt police, judges, and prosecutors impaired due process and the rule of law. Besides criminals and terrorists, human rights activists, left-wing political activists, and Muslims were sometimes the victims of improper police conduct. Violence against women and abuse of children remained serious problems, and some children were pressed into slave labor and prostitution.